1988
Samuel and J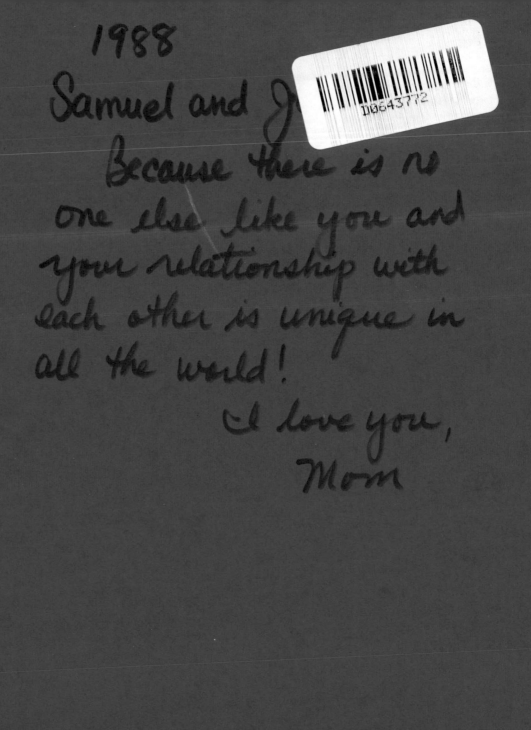
   Because there is no
one else like you and
your relationship with
each other is unique in
all the world!

      I love you,
        Mom

Being | Having
a Twin, | a Twin

Lothrop, Lee & Shepard Books
New York

Being a Twin, Having a Twin

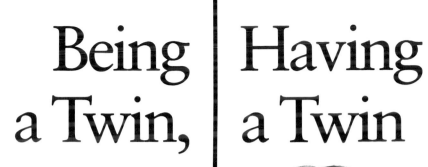

by Maxine B. Rosenberg

Photographs by
George Ancona

Library of Congress Cataloging in Publication Data
Rosenberg, Maxine B.
Being a twin, having a twin.
Summary: Describes the experiences of several different sets of twins,
both identical and fraternal.
1. Twins—Juvenile literature. [1. Twins] I. Ancona, George,
ill. II. Title
HQ777.35.R67 1985 155.4'44 84-17159
ISBN 0-688-04328-3   ISBN 0-688-04329-1 (lib. bdg.)

To my sister, Fran—
not my twin, but a best friend
—M.B.R.

To Ann Troy
—G.A.

"It's a boy.
What's this?
It's another boy!"

Peter and Matthew love to hear their mom tell them about the day they were born. All births are special, but Peter's and Matthew's were extra exciting, for the brothers were born on the same day. Six-year-old Peter and Matthew are twins.

It's unusual for humans to have more than one baby at a time. In fact, doctors say that for every 89 births, 88 will be just one child and one will be twins. And much less often, "supertwins," or three to six babies, are born at a time. But that rarely happens.

About two-thirds of all twins are fraternals, like Katy and Jimmy, age 6½ . . .

and Alison and Betsy, age 8. Fraternal twins do not look alike, and they are no more the same than any other brothers or sisters in their family.

When most people talk about twins, though, they talk about identicals. Identical twins are exactly alike in almost every way. They are the same sex. They have the same color hair and eyes, and the same shaped face and body-build. When they grow up, they'll be the same size. Usually they like the same foods, and many times, they get sick on the same day.

Peter and Matthew are identical twins. So are Patty and Jenny, age 9. Because they are identical, it's easy to confuse one for the other or to forget who's who. Instead, people may call each of them "twinny" or lump them together as "the twins."

To make it easier to tell them apart, Patty and Jenny got different haircuts. Even so, some people never try to find out what makes each girl special.

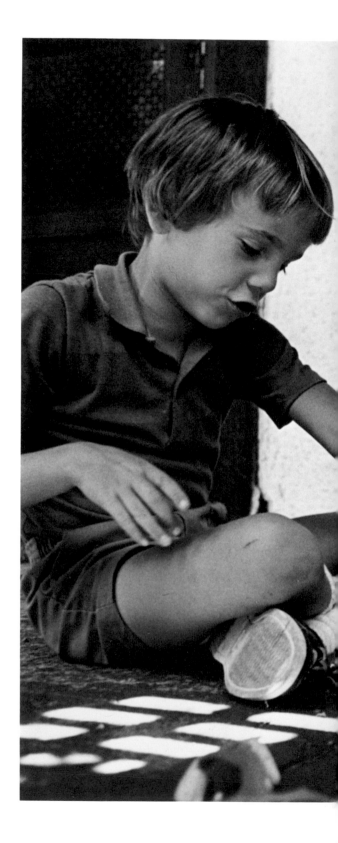

Matthew offers a clue that his friend uses to know which brother is which. "Christian's played with us a billion years, and so he picks us out by our voices."

Still, there is confusion. Sometimes even parents get mixed up.

"My dad says, 'Matthew, come and pick up your stuff,' " says Peter, laughing. "I have to tell him 'I'm not Matthew, Dad; I'm Peter.' "

Fraternal twins like Alison and Betsy and Katy and Jimmy don't have the look-alike problems of identicals. However, because they're twins they do share the same birthday,

just as Peter and Matthew and Patty and Jenny do. And being the same age and living in the same family, they've learned to share more than other brothers and sisters.

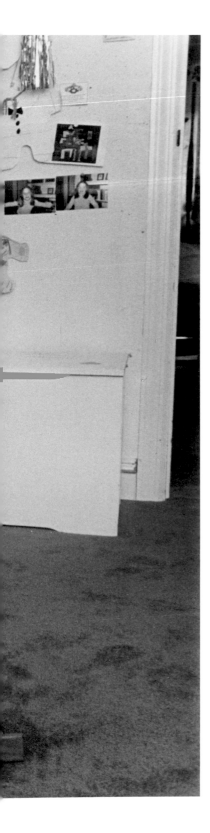

When they are young, twins usually share the same room, the same carriage, and the same toys. And having only one mother and father, identicals and fraternals may have to share the time spent with their parents. As they get older, they may make the same friends and have to share them too.

"Alison and I both like Annie, but we hardly get to play with her alone," says Betsy. "Annie invites the two of us to her house together so that neither of us will be hurt."

"I wish Annie and I could play without Betsy," whispers Alison.

Since they are of opposite sexes, Katy and Jimmy have different friends. On the weekends though, they like to go tree-climbing together or build a castle with their dad. Often Jimmy and his dad construct enormous skyscrapers.

"I don't like doing that," says Katy, "and so I sit near them and watch."

Jimmy, however, wishes Katy wouldn't hang around at all. He'd like his dad all to himself.

"If I was ten," he moans, "I'd get to stay up late and watch TV with Mommy and Daddy. Then Katy would be the baby and have to go to bed early."

With identicals, spending time together is less of a problem, for they are each other's best friends. Although identicals like other people, their twin is the person they usually choose to be with, especially when they're young. Identicals are born with this special feeling for each other. Not only do they want to be together, but also they are upset when they are apart.

"Last week Matthew threw a pretzel at me," confides Peter. "Mommy sent him to his room. She didn't know I sneaked upstairs and kept him company."

Patty and Jenny have not been in the same class since kindergarten. Even so, they still miss each other and often stop to hug in the hallway.

Now, when Peter and Matthew play, they run through their house as a twosome. If Matthew goes to the bathroom, Peter follows. If Peter starts building a tunnel, Matthew works on the tollbooth. It's as if each can read the other's mind.

To express their feelings, identical twins often make the same faces. Sometimes they finish each other's sentences before anyone can guess what is going to be said.

When Peter and Matthew were three years old, they, like many identicals, had their own private language. And even today, they still use words no one else can understand. "Himahama," they shout, jumping up and down.

In addition to these special links, identicals usually have the ability to do equally well in the same activities. This makes it easy for each to enjoy the other's company because it means they often have similar interests. For instance, if one twin swims well, the other probably can too. And if one identical is talented in dancing, most likely the other will have the same talent. How well each twin does depends on how hard she tries or how he feels.

Patty and Jenny are both great in gymnastics, but because Jenny is braver, she can do better flips on the trampoline. Although Jenny helps her sister, Patty is still frightened she'll fall off.

"Kids ask why I'm not as good as my twin sister," says Patty. "That makes me sad."

Peter doesn't like it either when others compare him to Matthew. He isn't as daring as his brother, especially on his bicycle. But Matthew doesn't have the patience to be the artist Peter is.

Sometimes one identical twin may start an activity first and become good at it. The other twin, afraid of never catching up, may even refuse to try. This almost happened to Patty and Jenny. Patty began piano lessons before her sister. By the time Jenny started lessons two years later, Patty was far ahead of her.

"In the beginning I wouldn't practice," says Jenny, "because I knew Patty would always be the best."

Luckily Jenny had a different teacher, who never talked about Patty's talent. And Patty was always ready to help whenever Jenny had a problem with the music. Now, although Patty is still the better musician, the sisters can play duets together.

Both identical and fraternal twins agree that the best part about being a twin is always having someone around who is the same age. In the morning, Matthew and Peter are particularly happy to have each other as they wait for the school bus. And Alison and Betsy admit it was easier starting Sunday school as a team than going there alone.

"I was scared the first time," confesses Alison, "especially when a boy started bothering me. But Betsy told him, 'Don't do that to my sister. It's not nice,' and he stopped. I'm glad she was there."

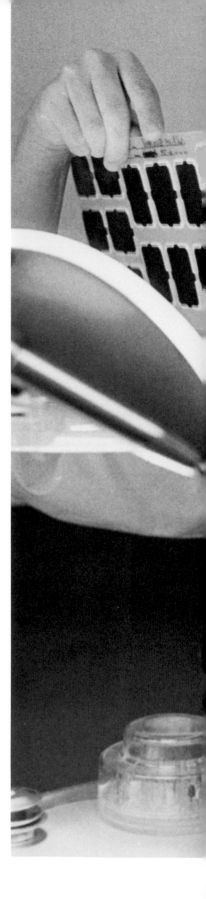

Because fraternal and identical twins are often together, they come to protect one another more than most brothers and sisters. Even as grown-ups, they continue to help each other out and think of the other as a good friend. In fact, it isn't unusual for adult identicals to live near each other or work together. Often they say their twin is the one who understands them best—more than their mother or father, or a husband or wife. Although they may be miles apart, many say they can tell when the other is hurt or in serious trouble.

Identical twins usually care for one another more deeply than fraternals. This is because of the special bond between them that grew even as they were inside their mother. However, after being a tight twosome as young children, around their ninth or tenth birthday, identicals often choose to be apart more. This helps them feel like they're two separate people.

Patty and Jenny, for example, no longer share a room. Yet, many mornings their dad finds them snuggled in the same bed. They've also stopped having one large birthday party on the same day. Patty has a lunch for her friends, while Jenny prefers a sleep-over. Each, however, helps the other plan the games and serve the food.

By the time identical twins are in high school, they usually spend less time together. That's when they start making new friends and discovering their own special interests. If they ever dressed alike, they rarely do anymore. But the caring and love for each other remains so that as they get older, they often choose to be near each other again.

Fraternal or identical, being a twin means having someone special in your life forever.

"It makes sharing more fun," says Alison. "And if you're a twin, you're never lonely," adds Betsy.

About Twins

Of all twins born, more than half are boys. As with singletons (children who are born one at a time), though, girls have a better rate of survival. For fraternal twins, race and heredity are important factors. Worldwide, the largest groups bearing fraternals are blacks and American Indians, with Asians reporting the fewest. However, twins are considered bad luck among the Chinese and Japanese, and so the statistics for Asians may not be accurate. In addition, advancing age of the mother (35–40 years old) and an increasing number of pregnancies can make fraternal twin births more likely. By contrast, identical twins are the result of chance—race, heredity, and age do not play a part. In the United States, twin births, both fraternal and identical, are on the rise as women delay pregnancy until they are older and resort more readily to fertility pills.

Identical twins are formed when a single fertilized egg divides into two replicas of itself. Although the genes for each half are the same, identical genes rarely produce completely identical results. This accounts for the slight variations, such as in finger, hand, and footprints, that scientists use to distinguish identical twins from one another. By contrast, fraternal twins are formed when two sperms fertilize two separate eggs. In this case no ovum—and therefore no gene material—is shared. Thus fraternal twins are biologically no different from singletons; they are simply siblings born at the same time.

In 1974, in Rome, the city which is said to have been founded by the mythological twins Romulus and Remus, the International Society of Twin Studies was formed. One of their goals was to utilize twin psychology as a tool in helping to understand the behavior patterns of couples in all relationships. Also by sharing medical research on twins, scientists could more easily determine which human diseases are inherited. Over the last ten years, three congresses have been held. Contrary to popular belief, their studies indicate that a person's susceptibility to measles, chicken pox, and rubella is probably inherited. On the other hand, there is little to prove that personality traits—as opposed to talents and skills—of individuals are passed through the genes. Twins, no doubt, hold the key to many unanswered questions about human physical well-being and behavior patterns.